MW01283031

The Naked Truth

By: Rich Orloff

Rebel Belle Publishing

The Naked Truth Copyright © 2017 Rich Orloff All Rights Reserved

Any THE NAKED TRUTH posters or other form of advertising, programs, online information and all other forms of publicity must include "produced by special arrangement with Rebel Belle Publishing." The English language stock and amateur stage performance rights in the United States, its territories, possessions and Canada for THE NAKED TRUTH are controlled exclusively by Rebel Belle Publishing, 720 Guy Jarrard Rd., Dahlonega, GA 30533. No professional or non-professional performance of the Play may be given without obtaining in advance the written permission of Rebel Belle Publishing, and paying the requisite fee. Professionals and amateurs are warned that performance of THE NAKED TRUTH is subject to payment of a royalty. It is fully protected under the copyright laws of the United States of America, and of all countries covered by the International Copyright Union (including the Dominion of Canada and the rest of the British Commonwealth), and of all countries covered by the Pan-American Copyright Convention, the Universal Copyright Convention, the Berne Convention, and all of the countries with which the United States has reciprocal copyright relations. All rights, including without limitation professional/amateur stage rights, motion picture, recitation, lecturing, public reading, radio broadcasting, television, video or sound recording, all other forms of mechanical, electronic and digital reproduction, transmission and distribution, such as CD, DVD, the Internet, private and file sharing networks, information storage and retrieval systems, photocopying, and the rights of translation into foreign languages are strictly reserved. Particular emphasis is placed upon the matter of readings, permission for which must be secured from the Authors' agent in writing.
Inquiries concerning all other rights should be addressed to the author c/o Rebel Belle Publishing, 720 Guy Jarrard Rd., Dahlonega, GA 30533.
Anyone receiving permission to produce THE NAKED TRUTH is required to give credit to the Author as sole and exclusive Author of the Play on the title page of all programs distributed in connection with performances of the Play and in all instances in which the title of the Play appears for purposes of advertising, publicizing or otherwise exploiting the Play and/or a production thereof. The names of the author must appear on a separate line in which no other name appears, immediately beneath the title and in size of type equal to 50% of the size of the largest, most prominent letter used for the title of the Play. No person, firm or entity may receive credit larger or more prominent than that accorded the author.
The logo for THE NAKED TRUTH, available for download at www.RebelBellePublishing.com, is required for use in all playbills, posters and other promotional materials.

THE NAKED TRUTH

a comedy

Characters

CLARK, 30 (or so), the front desk clerk at the Godiva Inn

GEORGE, 40's, the new owner

LIZ, 40's, his wife

JANE, 30's, the inn's handyman

FRED, 40's (or so), a hotel chain representative

plus the off-stage voices of a few hotel guests

Place

The lobby of a small inn on Key West, Florida

Time

The present

THE NAKED TRUTH

SCENE ONE

The lobby of the Godiva Inn, a small resort in Key West. Although this place has seen better days, it's been kept in decent shape. There's a door on one side of the lobby to the rest of the resort and a door on the other side to the rest of the world. Between these doors is a door to an apartment for the owner-manager. There's a counter, behind which the staff works. The lobby is decorated with tropical colors, and the furnishings include a couch, chairs, a table with a coffee pot and accoutrements, and a brochure stand.

CLARK, the resort's clerk, stands behind the counter. Flamboyant and sharp, Clark has seen it all, and he wishes he had taken photos. The phone rings.

>   CLARK
>   (into the phone:)
>   Godiva Inn, where every guest is barely
>   dressed... Yes, we're a clothing-optional resort...
>   No, I'm not naked... Because my body
>   is a temple, and it's only open on religious
>   holidays... No, you can't be naked in the
>   lobby, just around the pool and hot tub,
>   which we clean daily – *we have our reasons.*

Another line rings.

>   CLARK (cont'd)
>   Will you hold a second?

(switches to other line, and:)
Godiva Inn, where every woman and man
gets a full-body tan... I said I'll pay you!...
As soon as I pay everyone else!... Well, stop
thinking of it as money, and start thinking
of it as your contribution to art... Well,
if that's how you feel, you should've
never gone into the sequin business!
(switches lines, and tone:)
Thank you for holding... I'd be glad to
make a reservation for you... I'll check...
Yes, we have a few rooms free that night.
Do you prefer smoking, non-smoking,
or "*I* don't smoke, but if I end up with
two smokin' hotties *I'll* supply the match."

Another line rings.

CLARK (cont'd)
One moment.
(switches lines:)
Godiva Inn, where the thin and stout like
to flesh it out... Of course, I plan to pay you...
Well, not that soon... Not that soon... I plan
to be reincarnated. Ask me in my next life.
(switches lines, and tone:)
Sorry for the interruption. Will this be
your first time in Key West?... Oh, you'll
love it. Key West is like Disneyland with
a libido... Now to hold your room, I'll need
your address and a credit card number...

On the last sentence, JANE has entered. Jane is the inn's
handyman, a job she loves because she gets to wear a tool belt.

                    JANE
    I fixed the faucet in Number Eight.

                    CLARK
                (into the phone:)
    And the card number?

Jane notices a hang nail. She tries to bite it off, unsuccessfully.
So she uses her wire cutters on it. She blows on the wire
cutters
as if it were a gun, and she puts it back in her belt.

                    CLARK (cont'd)
    Expiration date? You're all set...
    See you in a few weeks.

Clark hangs up.

                    JANE
        Any word from –

                    CLARK
    Jane, can you lend me ohhhhh
    twenty-thirty thousand dollars till payday?

                    JANE
    If I could, do you think I'd be working two jobs?

                    CLARK
    What am I going to do, Jane?
    Creditors are calling me day and night.

                    JANE
    Well, maybe you should stop spending
    so much money on your hobby.

CLARK

Being a drag queen is *not* a hobby! It's my *art*.

JANE

Then stop thinking of it as an art
and turn it into a hobby.

CLARK

Oh, what am I going to do?

JANE

Have faith.

CLARK

I *do* have faith. I have faith that one day
I will be the Sarah Bernhardt of drag queens.
I will be the Duse of Drag. I'll be the
greatest female impersonator since
Tallulah Bankhead impersonated herself.

JANE

Shouldn't they be here by now?

CLARK

I don't want to think about them.

JANE

You're going to have to. Their car
should be pulling up any –

CLARK

I doubt it. I bet they'll stop at every key
along the way, going, "Look darling, in
Florida they call their islands *keys*. Isn't
that *cute*? Let's put one in our trunk."

                    JANE
Are you going to be nice to them?

                    CLARK
I don't see why I should be.

                    JANE
Because Roger asked you to be.

                    CLARK
They didn't even come to his funeral.

                    JANE
They weren't invited.

                    CLARK
If I only went to places I was invited,
I'd be a hermit.

                    JANE
Do you think folks would've been
comfortable with them at the funeral?

                    CLARK
If they dressed up in drag.

                    JANE
Clark.

                    CLARK
A boa. One boa.

                    JANE
Look, just because Roger's brother
wasn't accepting of hi—

CLARK
No. "Not accepting" is like "This dress
is *lovely*, but it makes my ass look big."
Rejecting your brother is –

JANE
You don't talk to *your* brother.

CLARK
My brother's an asshole.
A big asshole. A *huge* asshole.

JANE
Okay.

CLARK
There's like a Grand Canyon between his cheeks.

JANE
Well, Roger never described his brother
or sister-in-law as assholes.

CLARK
Well, you see, there's another problem.

JANE
What?

CLARK
His brother's married. You know what that
means?

JANE
What?

CLARK

There's a two-thirds chance he's straight.

JANE

Hey, don't knock married men. My other job
would vanish if it weren't for married men.
They're dependable, they pay on time,
and they're totally grateful for my services.

CLARK

Well, I guess you've had better luck with
married men than I have. All the secrecy, the
deception. No more, you hear me, no more! If
you can't be straight with your wife – you can't
be gay with me.

JANE

Admit it, Clark. You're a heterophobe.

CLARK

I am not. Some of my best friends
are straight people.

JANE

Name five.

CLARK

I didn't say "a lot".

JANE

Well, just remember what Roger asked us.

CLARK

I will.

> JANE

On his deathbed.

> CLARK

I will bathe them in lovingkindness,
and squeeze the sponge.

Jane's cellphone rings. She answers it.

> JANE

Mistress Dominique. Speak... Well, how much
do you want it?... Is that all? Tell how much
you *really* want it...

Clark imitates a begging dog, whining softly, barking, and
panting.
Jane nonchalantly takes a newspaper and swats him.

> JANE (cont'd)

Okay, I'll meet you in a half-hour... 'Bye.

GEORGE and LIZ enter. Both in their forties, they're clean-
cut, model citizens, although not necessarily this year's model.
They carry some luggage.

> CLARK

Hello, may we help you?

> GEORGE

Is this the Godiva Inn?

> CLARK

No, it's Key West Hospital. Take off
your clothes and say "Ahhhh".

GEORGE

Um –

JANE

You must be Roger's brother.

GEORGE

Yes, hi, George Drummond.
And this is my wife Liz.

LIZ

Nice to meet you.

JANE

I'm the handyman, Jane.

CLARK

And I'm Clark, the hotel's clerk and concierge.
You have an "erge", I'll conci it.

GEORGE

Well, it's, it's nice meeting both of you.

JANE

How was your drive?

GEORGE

Exhausting.

LIZ

Our car barely made it.

JANE

I'll be glad to look at it if you like.

GEORGE
You know your way under the hood?

JANE
That's what my girlfriend says.
(George and Liz freeze.)
Oh, I forgot. You're from Ohio.

GEORGE
By the way, I, um, stopped at a gas station
for directions here and was told that this
place was um "clothing optional". By, by
any chance does that mean like – "casual"?

JANE
Didn't Roger tell you two about this place?

LIZ
Tell us what?

CLARK
Why do you think it's called the Godiva Inn?

GEORGE
Because staying here's like eating a fancy
chocolate?

JANE
Well, some of our guests *love* chocolate syrup.

CLARK
But only when they're covered in it.

JANE

So Roger didn't tell you –

GEORGE

Well, he and I, we didn't um –

LIZ

So this is like a nudist resort?

JANE

We prefer the phrase "clothing optional".

CLARK

Adults only.

GEORGE

And what do these "adults only" do here?

JANE

I don't ask; I don't tell.

CLARK

I ask; I tell.

JANE

I assure you the people here are 98% wholesome.

LIZ

And the other 2%?

CLARK

They're my favorite customers.

GEORGE

You mean, more goes on here than just nudity?

                                    LIZ
              George, that's probably true of every hotel.

From the pool area, we hear:

                              FEMALE HOTEL GUEST
(o.s.)

              Anybody got a spare condom?!

                                  GEORGE
              I've never heard that at a Holiday Inn.

                                   CLARK
              Look, anything that happens here has to
              be between two or more consenting adults.

                                   JANE
              And no animals.

                                   CLARK
              Remember when we had to kick out
              the guy with the sheep?

                                   JANE
              She was such a cute little sheep.
              With those little white curls.

                                   CLARK
              Just like my grandmother, except less
              judgmental.

Clark and Jane sigh.

                                  GEORGE
              I knew it was a mistake coming here.

LIZ

George.

GEORGE

We've had good lives in Dayton.

LIZ

Had, George, *had*.

GEORGE

When the lawyer told me Roger   left me this
place –

CLARK

He *what?!*

GEORGE

Didn't Roger or the lawyer tell you two that we

–

JANE

You're not just visiting?

CLARK

You own my, my *sanctuary*?

GEORGE

Don't worry. I plan to sell it.

LIZ

You promised it'd be a joint decision.

GEORGE

But Liz, this place sounds like a,
a non-stop orgy.

                    JANE
This place is *not* a non-stop orgy.

                    CLARK
Except of course, during Non-Stop Orgy Week.

                    JANE
And, I guess, Fantasy Fest –

                    CLARK
Mardi Gras –

                    JANE
And months ending in R or Y.

                    CLARK
Visit during hurricane season; it's dullsville.

                    LIZ
Oh, I get it. You're pulling our leg.

                    JANE
Clark will pull anything people let him.

                    GEORGE
So then this *isn't* a nudist resort?

From poolside, we hear:

                    ANOTHER HOTEL GUEST
(o.s.)
Anybody have any peanut butter – or KY jelly?!!!

                    GEORGE
We're selling.

                    17

LIZ
You promise we'd give it some time.

GEORGE
Aren't you aghast about what goes on here?

LIZ
I'm completely aghast, and slightly intrigued.

JANE
I like her.

GEORGE
And what if our kids find out
we're connected to this place?

LIZ
Then for the first time in our lives
they'll think we're interesting.

JANE
You have kids?

LIZ
A boy and a girl, both in college.

JANE
That must cost a mint.

LIZ
Plus some.

GEORGE
If you don't believe us, ask our creditors.
All our creditors.

                    CLARK
Bonding. I sense bonding!

                    JANE
            (checking her watch:)
Oh crap, I gotta run.

                    GEORGE
            (checking his watch:)
Are you already done for the day?

                    JANE
I'll be back in an hour-and-a-half or so.

                    GEORGE
Where are you going?

                    JANE
When I come back, I'll show you all
around the premises. Nice meeting you.

Jane rushes out.

                    GEORGE
Roger let his employees just take off like that?

                    CLARK
Well, you see, Key West is such an
expensive place to live; it's hard to
make ends meet with just one job.

                    GEORGE
What's her other job?

                    CLARK
Um, customer relations.

LIZ
Do you have a second job?

CLARK
Of course.

GEORGE
What kind of job?

CLARK
I'm an entertainer.

GEORGE
What kind of entertainer?

CLARK
Fabulous.

GEORGE
What kind of fabulous?

CLARK
Totally fabulous.

GEORGE
What kind of –

LIZ
George, maybe we should unpack
and settle in first.

CLARK

I guess you'll want to stay in
the owner-manager's suite.

LIZ

Is that where Roger lived?

CLARK

Yep. It's what he called home.

LIZ

George?

GEORGE

Yeah, I guess that's where we'll stay.
Clark, will you help us with our bags?

CLARK

Oh, no, I'm sorry, I don't do that.

GEORGE

You don't?

CLARK

I did that once and broke a nail.

George and Liz pick up their bags and start to exit.

LIZ

Welcome to Key West, darling.

CLARK

You'll love his suite. It has a view of everything.
(particularly to George:)
And I mean *evvverything*.

They exit into Roger's suite.

The lights fade.

SCENE TWO

The next morning. Clark cleans the coffee area when the phone rings.

> CLARK
> (into the phone:)
> Godiva Inn, where people sin wearing nothing but skin... Well, most of our guests are straight, but we do have weeks set aside for *every* lifestyle. So what's *your* inclination?... Oh, I remember you. And how's your sheep?... I'm sorry, but you know our policy: No animals. Just people. And select vegetables.

George enters, wearing a blazer, white shirt, and shorts. He gets some coffee.

> CLARK (cont'd)
> 'Bye.
> (hangs up phone.)
> Good morning.

> GEORGE
> (not in a good mood)
> Good morning.

> CLARK
> Rough first night in the tropics?

> GEORGE
> Is – is it like that around the pool every night?

                    CLARK
That depends. You'll have to tell me
what it was like – in detail.

                    GEORGE
It was like a human jigsaw puzzle.
And some of the pieces didn't even fit right.

                    CLARK
Well, it's not like that every night.

                    GEORGE
Oh, good.

                    CLARK
When it rains, the action moves indoors.

                    GEORGE
Are all clothing-optional resorts like this?

                    CLARK
Oh no no no. Most of them are filled with
respectable people who want to do nothing
more than lie nude under the sun and
who have no naughty thoughts whatsoever.

                    GEORGE
Really?

                    CLARK
Yep. There are naked Republicans.

                    GEORGE
I see.

George sips his coffee. Clark looks at him.

CLARK

George, why are you dressed like that?

GEORGE

Like what?

CLARK

Like you're going clubbing and tonight's theme is "Catholic school boy".

GEORGE

Am I overdressed?

CLARK

At this place, a thong is overdressed.

GEORGE

I just think that if I'm, even temporarily, management...

CLARK

Roger never dressed like that. Except when he went clubbing on "Catholic school boy night."

GEORGE

I'm not Roger.

CLARK

I've noticed. But as long as you're here, go a little Key West. Wear a flowery shirt.

GEORGE

But I'm not a, a –

CLARK

A what?

GEORGE

A, a flowery guy.

CLARK

George, anyone who spends two minutes with
you will know you don't have *any* chlorophyll.
Besides, you never know about folks. Would
you have guessed that I'm 20% heterosexual?

GEORGE

Twenty per cent?

CLARK

I was at an orgy once, and I learned
that if I'm having sex with ten people,
two of them can be women.

Liz enters. She's dressed a bit more appropriately for the
climate, but nothing flashy.

LIZ

Good morning.

CLARK

Good morning.

LIZ

Good morning, sweetie.

Liz and George kiss.

GEORGE

Good morning.

LIZ

Wasn't last night... fascinating?

GEORGE

I thought you went to sleep early.

LIZ

I woke up. Then I looked out. Then
I couldn't go back to sleep. Then I
didn't want to go back to sleep.

GEORGE

But, but I thought you were disgusted by them.

LIZ

Well, I was at first. Completely disgusted.
But the longer I looked, the more
I learned something about myself.

GEORGE

What?

LIZ

I can have two conflicting feelings at the same
time.

GEORGE

Well, I can't. Those people, they
were doing everything imaginable.

LIZ

I can imagine one or two things
they weren't doing.

Clark grabs a secretary's pad and pen, sits near Liz, and readies his pen.

                    CLARK
          Go on.
                    (off Liz and George's look:)
          Or I could return to my chores.

                    GEORGE
          Thank you.

Clark picks up a tray of coffee mugs (or something like that) and exits.

                    GEORGE (cont'd)
          Liz, I'm, I'm shocked at what I'm hearing from
          you.

                    LIZ
          Well, it's nice to know that there can
          still be some surprises in our marriage.

                    GEORGE
          Honey, this place, it, it just isn't me.
          Dayton is me.

                    LIZ
          Sweetie, when we were walking around
          yesterday, I mean, I love our friends back
          home, but, but back home, people were
          happy because they got a job promotion,
          or their kids did well in school, or something
          happened. Here it's like, people seem to
          be happy for no apparent reason. I want
          to be happy for no apparent reason, George.

We both need to learn that skill.

GEORGE
You didn't like our life in Dayton?

LIZ
I *loved* our life in Dayton. But our kids are gone, our jobs are gone, and our house is almost gone. I think that love affair is over.

GEORGE
And, and what about *our* love affair?

LIZ
I love our marriage. And you. But last night, I don't know, it's – Have you ever wondered what's on the other side of what we allow ourselves to do?

GEORGE
No.

LIZ
Not even once?

GEORGE
No.

LIZ
Sweetie –

GEORGE
Honey, the people here...

LIZ
So some of them act a little wild.

I'm sure when they put on their clothes,
they're just like you and me.

Jane enters, in a dominatrix outfit.

JANE
Sorry I'm late. I had a breakfast meeting.

GEORGE
Is, is this the Key West version of Casual Friday?

JANE
Okay, I'll level with you.   I have a second job.

Clark returns during the above speech.

GEORGE
What's the the the job?

CLARK
She's a milkmaid. Specializing in whipped
cream.

JANE
I'm a part-time dominatrix. And don't
worry, I get everything done here
that needs to get done.

LIZ
Can, can I ask a personal question?

JANE
Ask me anything. My life's an open book.

CLARK
Bound in leather.

LIZ
Why did you become a –

JANE
Because working at this place doesn't pay
well enough to feed me and my daughter.

GEORGE
You have a daughter?

JANE
Back home. It's a long, sordid story.

CLARK
But a *good* long, sordid story.

JANE
You see, I used to be married.

GEORGE
So you used to be heterosexual?

JANE
Yep, been there, done that... You see, I
thought I fell in love with my husband because
he wore a tool belt. But it turns out I just loved
tool belts. Anyway, at the divorce trial the
judge decided that our daughter being raised
by a lesbian would corrupt her. But living with
a beer-guzzling, foul-mouthed cheatin' bigot
was keeping with community values.

GEORGE
Wow, that's quite a, wow.

JANE

And well, maybe I was having a few problems,
too. Anyway, I keep sending her checks 'cause,
well, my ex doesn't believe in spoiling her
with things like, you know, books.

LIZ

Does being a dominatrix pay well?

JANE

Oh, yeah.

GEORGE

Then why work here?

JANE

Because there are a limited number of men on
this island who like being beaten and
humiliated.

CLARK

I beg to differ.

JANE

And who can afford to pay for it.

CLARK

Well, that's true.

JANE
(to George, with strength)
So I'd like to keep my job here, but if
you can't handle me having another one...

LIZ

Well, sweetie?

GEORGE

Um, well, as long as you get your work done
here...

CLARK

And I'm not giving up my other job, either.

LIZ

Are *you* supporting a child?

Clark reacts as if the concept gives him a heart attack. Then:

CLARK

No. But I am the soul support
of several fabulous outfits.

GEORGE

Outfits?

CLARK

Dresses, evening gowns, and
one rhinestone pants suit.

GEORGE

So you're a transvestite?

CLARK

(deeply offended)

I am *not* a transvestite! I am a drag queen.

LIZ

What's the difference?

CLARK

"What's the difference?"! It's the difference

between flats and heels, floor wax and
getting waxed, being attractive and
being fabulous. Anyone can be a woman.
You need talent to become a diva.

GEORGE
Okay, it's 9:30, and I think I've had
enough surprises for the day.

CLARK
Not fair. We told you some of our secrets.
You have to tell us some of yours.

GEORGE
I need to start going over the books and things –

CLARK
Pleeeze?

LIZ
George and I both lost our jobs this past year –
his company was downsized and mine moved
to China – and so our kids could stay in college,
our credit cards are like maxxed out and
we have a double mortgage on our house.

JANE
Wow, that's intense.

CLARK
And concise.

JANE
You're actually risking your house
so your kids can stay in school?

GEORGE

We promised we'd put them through college, and, well, we promised.

CLARK

That's so, so – Will you two adopt me?

LIZ

I'm sorry. We're not paying for any more schooling.

CLARK

How about tap lessons?

GEORGE

I think we should all get to work.

CLARK
(to Jane:)
Should we give George the –

JANE

Not yet.

GEORGE

The what?

JANE and CLARK
(simultaneously:)
Nothing.

LIZ

I may go for a swim.

JANE

I better change.

Liz and Jane start to leave together.

> LIZ
> So you really do things like tie people up
> and spank them?

> JANE
> Uh-huh.

> LIZ
> Why?

> JANE
> I like working with my hands.

Liz and Jane exit.

> CLARK
> You know, I almost had a long-term
> relationship with a dominatrix once.

> GEORGE
> Really?

> CLARK
> But I wasn't ready to be tied down.

> GEORGE
> I should get back to work.

George exits.

> CLARK
> He still has a *lot* to learn.

Clark resumes work.

The lights fade.

SCENE THREE

A few mornings later. Clark is working. The phone rings.

> CLARK
> (into the phone:)
> Godiva Inn, where folks come back, 'cause
> they don't need to pack... Yes, I know how
> much I owe you... Yes, I know how long it's
> been... Well, if our government doesn't have
> to pay off *its* debt, I don't see why *I* have to!

Clark hangs up. George enters. He's still conservatively dressed,
but at least he's not wearing a tie. He looks like he's in shock.

> CLARK (cont'd)

You okay?

> GEORGE
> I just saw my wife *naked*.

> CLARK
> Well, after twenty years of marriage, I think it's

time.

> GEORGE
> No, I mean, in the pool. And then by the pool.
> Totally nude. Without any clothes.

CLARK

Like the day she was born.

GEORGE

No, I've seen pictures of the day she was born. They wrapped her up immediately.

CLARK

So what's the big deal?

GEORGE

There were other people there.

CLARK

Were they videotaping?

GEORGE

You have no shame, do you?

CLARK

Oh, I used to have plenty of shame, but I gave it up for Lent.

Liz enters, in a robe.

LIZ

You know, I love starting the day with a swim. Every day I'm here, I feel younger.

GEORGE

And I'm sure you've given some youthful ideas to other people, too.

LIZ

George, what's the matter?

GEORGE

I saw you naked in the pool.

LIZ

So?

GEORGE

So there were ten naked people
around the pool who could see you.

LIZ

One of them was wearing a cap.

GEORGE

Okay, nine naked people and a rabbi.

CLARK

Oh, I met him. We had a *fabulous*
chit-chat about foreskin. He's against
it, and I like being against it.

LIZ

George, every morning for the first
week we were here, I wore a swimsuit.
That's when I felt gawked at. If they
don't care if I'm naked, why should I?

GEORGE

But what if someone else was in the
pool and they touched your, your –

LIZ

Big toe?

GEORGE

No.

                         LIZ
Elbow?

                         GEORGE
No.

                         LIZ
Ankle?

                         GEORGE
No.

                         CLARK
Can I guess? Can I guess?
                 (off George and Liz's look:)
Well, if you're not going to let everyone play,
you shouldn't do this in public.

Clark exits.

                         GEORGE
Honey, I've been thinking, maybe, maybe
we should convert this place to a family hotel.

                         LIZ
This place does fine as it is.

                         GEORGE
But maybe it could do even better
if we attracted a different kind of –

                         LIZ
George, have you *talked* to any of our guests yet?

                         GEORGE
Of course.

LIZ

Besides telling them where the ice machine is.

GEORGE

No.

LIZ

You know, a lot of them are churchgoers.

GEORGE

There are clothing-optional churches?!

LIZ

That reminds me: Jane invited us
to go to church with her this Sunday.

GEORGE

Jane goes to church?

LIZ

Every Sunday.

GEORGE

You know, you, you've been spending
a lot of time with her.

LIZ

And I'm so grateful. She really knows
every nook and cranny in this town.

GEORGE

She's showing you her nooks and crannies?!

LIZ

Sweetie, what's the matter?

GEORGE

What if, what if she brings out
hidden feelings in you?

LIZ

Are you afraid I'll turn lesbian?

GEORGE

Who knows? I find women attractive;
why shouldn't you?

LIZ

I find men attractive; do you?

GEORGE

No, and to be honest, I've never
figured out why women do, either.

LIZ

I find you attractive.

GEORGE

Yeah, well that's the biggest mystery.

LIZ

What happened to you, George?

GEORGE

What do you mean?

LIZ

When we started out, you used to be fun.
Even a little naughty sometimes.

GEORGE
Really? Was *I* there when this happened?

LIZ
Oh, yeah. Remember when we were dating and
we –
    (She whispers in his ear.)
And when we –
    (She whispers in his ear.)
And when we –
    (She nibbles his ear.)

GEORGE
    (after she finishes:)
Remind me again.

LIZ
Well, then...

She nibbles his ear.

GEORGE
Ohh... Ohhh... More lobe. More lobe.

Liz nibbles George's ear more fervently. He responds. Clark
enters.

CLARK
Run out of Q-Tips?

GEORGE
Oh, well, uh –

LIZ
I think I'll get dressed.

GEORGE

Good idea.

Liz exits.

CLARK

You know, George, I know you have
a lot of critical opinions about our
guests, but you haven't exactly been
an angel around this place, either.

GEORGE

What do you mean?

CLARK

Yesterday, I saw you gawk at
that leggy gal with the great tan.

GEORGE

I *glanced* at her.

CLARK

It looked like a scene from the Bible.

GEORGE

What?

CLARK

You were worshipping her golden calves.

Jane enters, in her handyman outfit.

JANE

Congratulations, George. As of this moment,
all of your pipes are in great shape. Unless
you also have one for recreational purposes.

                    (off George's look:)
          Prrrrobably not.

The phone rings.

                         CLARK
          Godiva Inn. Where a thing of beauty
          has a naked booty... When?!...
          Where?!... I'll be right there!

Clark hangs up and starts to rush out the door.

                         CLARK (cont'd)
          I'll be back in half-an-hour. One
          of you will have to cover for me.

                         GEORGE
          Is something the matter?

                         CLARK
          Someone spotted somebody at the
          Sheraton who looks like Anderson Cooper.

Clark exits.

                         GEORGE
          Um –

                         JANE
          I can handle the front desk.

                         GEORGE
          Thanks. Oh, um, Liz told me
          you've invited us to Sunday –

JANE

I hope you'll join us. It's an amazing service.
And you'll love our minister. She's great.

GEORGE

"She"?

JANE
(a bit intimidating)
You have a problem with that?

GEORGE

Not out loud.

JANE

Great. Oh, I have to take off at about
three for a business appointment.

GEORGE

As a –

JANE

Behavioral therapist.

GEORGE

People really pay you to give them pain?

JANE

You bet.

GEORGE

Really?

JANE

If they don't pay, I don't punish them.

GEORGE

And during a, a –

JANE

Session –

GEORGE

You just keep going until they say "No"?

JANE

Oh, no.

GEORGE

No?

JANE

In the S&M world, "No" can mean "Yes".

GEORGE

Oh. Do they say "Stop"?

JANE

No, "stop" can mean "more".

GEORGE

What about "That hurts!"

JANE

That can mean a big tip.

GEORGE

Then how can they tell you they've had enough?

JANE

You use a code word.

GEORGE

A code word?

JANE

Something that wouldn't be part of a regular
S&M conversation. Like a color, or a vegetable.

GEORGE

Oh. So like people yell out "Carrot!"

Liz enters, unseen by George and Jane.

JANE

Right. Or "Tomato!"

GEORGE

Or "Zucchini!"

JANE

Or "Eggplant!"

LIZ

Although depending on your fetish,
you probably shouldn't yell "Squash!"

GEORGE

I've got work to do.

JANE

See you later.

LIZ

See you later, sweetie.

GEORGE

I'll never be able to look at a salad again.

George exits.

LIZ

Poor guy.

JANE

What do you mean?

LIZ

It's just, well, he was raised a certain way,
and he's always tried to be a certain way,
and he's wanted me to be a certain way,
and he wants the world to be a certain way.
He has very high, very dull standards.

JANE

And you?

LIZ

And he's a loving father, and he cares
the world about me, and he's a good man.

JANE

And you?

LIZ

He's really been a bedrock in hard times.

JANE

And you?

LIZ

If I wanted to answer the question, I would've.

JANE

Hey, don't worry about it. My girl friend Midge
and I have had our ups and downs, too. There
have been at least two dozen times when I've
wanted to call it quits. But we keep working at
it, and communicating, and listening, and
forgiving, and that's how we get through the
hard times.

LIZ

How long have you two been together?

JANE

Three weeks.

LIZ

Where'd you meet, at some cool lesbian hot
spot?

JANE

Yep. A twelve-step meeting.

LIZ

Are you an –

JANE

Al Anon.

LIZ

Oh.

JANE

My ex liked to drink. It made him
feel like a man: numb and oblivious.

LIZ

I see.

JANE

You'll have to meet Midge. She's just great.

LIZ

I'd love to meet her.

JANE

Of course, since I've started spending time
with you, she's become like totally jealous.

LIZ

But I'm straight.

JANE

To Midge, all straight people are closet
bisexuals, and all bisexuals are closet homos.

LIZ

I'm sorry, if I –

JANE

Don't apologize. Ever since Midge started
jealous and suspicious, she's been giving me
double the pleasure. And double the gums.

LIZ

Oh, well, that's good I guess.

JANE

That's what I like best about sex with a woman.
Unlike my ex, when Midge is in the driver's seat,
she's always willing to take the scenic route.
        (then:)

My husband liked to floor it.

                    LIZ
Oh, my.

                    JANE
So if I can –

                    LIZ
Sure.

                    JANE
How's George in the –

                    LIZ
He's a dependable driver.

                    JANE
I'm glad.

                    LIZ
Never speeds, never passes without signaling.

                    JANE
That's great.

                    LIZ
For over twenty years, I can count on him
to successfully take me down the same road,
the very same road, the very very same road.
Between you and me, for years I've been
praying for a pothole.

                    JANE
Maybe that's why God wants you in Key West.

LIZ

That's why I like you, Jane. Your God
is all-knowing, all-seeing and all-kinky.

JANE

Well, I don't kn–

LIZ

And speaking of cars, well, I really
appreciate you teaching me how to
change my oil and lubricate my engine.

JANE

I'm always glad to share what I've learned.

Unseen by the women, George enters.

LIZ

Since knowing you, my engine's
running better than ever.

JANE

Well, when you're as eager to learn
as you are, lubricating is easy.

LIZ

It's because you're a great teacher.

JANE

Hey, all you need for happiness is
fifteen minutes and the right oil.

LIZ

I'm just glad I don't have to go to
professionals anymore. Thank you.

JANE
Hey, I should be thanking you. Like I said,
'cause of you: climax, climax, climax!

George begins to cough.

LIZ
George, are you okay?

GEORGE
I have a little something in my throat.

JANE
That's what I used to call sex with my husband.

LIZ
George, you don't look good.

GEORGE
I'm fine, I'm fine. But I've just made a decision.

LIZ
George?

GEORGE
It'll be good for this place, it'll be good
for our marriage, and it'll probably
even be good for Key West.

LIZ
What will?

GEORGE
I'm renaming this place: The Snow White Inn!

George exits. Liz and Jane look at each other.

The lights fade.

SCENE FOUR

A week later. Clark is at front desk. His clothing is *very* straight,
but his eyes seem a bit, well, enhanced. Perhaps some mascara
and false eyelashes, possibly more. The phone rings.

> CLARK
> Snow White Inn. Where we aim to please
> without a trace of sleaze... No, we don't allow
> that anymore... We don't allow that either...
> We never allowed that, but could you describe
> that again *slowly*?... Well, we have a new
> concept now. Our place is for people who
> want to visit Florida but still feel surrounded
> by Ohio... Well, I'm sorry, too. Goodbye.

George has entered during the end of the call.

> GEORGE
> So how's it – um, Clark, is – is there
> something different about your eyes?

> CLARK
> It's my homage to Snow White's eyes,
> what do you think?

                    GEORGE
Clark –

                    CLARK
You want this place to go Disney, don't you?

                    GEORGE
Clark –

                    CLARK
Look, I'm getting all my work done, and
nobody's batted an eyelash... except me.

Clark bats his eyelashes.

                    GEORGE
If I hear a *single* complaint –

                    CLARK
Deal.

                    GEORGE
             (referring to work and glad
             to change the subject:)
So – how's it going?

                    CLARK
Every time I talk to a former guest,
I feel like I'm notifying the next-of-kin.

                    GEORGE
I know it's slow now, but once we develop
a new clientele –

                    CLARK
You know, Roger put his heart and soul into this
place.

GEORGE

I'm not Roger.

CLARK

That's for sure.

GEORGE

You know, I don't like being judged.

CLARK

Well, aren't you judging all the people
who like this place as it is?

GEORGE

Damn it, irresponsible sexual behavior
can *kill* people.

CLARK

Roger wasn't irresponsible, George.

GEORGE

Well, maybe you and I define irresponsible –

CLARK

He was fun but not irresponsible.

GEORGE

Then how'd he get Hepatitis C?

CLARK

What?

GEORGE

How'd he get Hepatitis C?

CLARK

Wasn't Roger in an accident as a kid?

                    GEORGE

Yeah, a car hit him when he was riding a bike.
So?

                    CLARK

And he needed blood, right?

                    GEORGE

Yeah, so?

                    CLARK

Sooo... Roger told me Hep C can take
25-30 years to affect someone. And they
didn't test blood for Hep C thirty years ago.
                (after a long silence:)
George?

                    GEORGE

I, I just assumed...

                    CLARK

Of course you did.

                    GEORGE

It's just I... I always figured that,
that we'd both live long enough that...
that one day we'd make up.

                    CLARK

I'm sorry.

Jane enters, in work clothes. She carries a clipboard.

                    JANE

Well I –

(noticing Clark's eyes:)
Ooo, I like your long lashes.

CLARK

I'm sure your clients say the same thing.

JANE

Well, George, I finished making sure all the
changes you wanted were implemented.

GEORGE

Oh, that's... that's great.

JANE

(saddened by the changes:)
The TV sets can no longer get adult
programming,
the vending machine no longer dispenses
condoms,
and the pool no longer has inflatable sex dolls.

GEORGE

I'm glad.

JANE

As of this moment, I think it's safe to say
this place has been successfully neutered.

Liz enters. She wears a tool belt and handyman clothes.

LIZ

Well, I put up the sign by the hot tub saying no
obscene behavior or anything that might cause
bubbles.
(noticing Clark's eyes:)
Nice.

CLARK

Thanks.

GEORGE

Um, Liz.

LIZ

Uh-huh.

GEORGE

Have you been, uh...
                    (indicating her outfit:)
shopping.

LIZ

Uh-huh. What do you think?

CLARK

I think it's *fabulous*.

JANE

So do I.

GEORGE

I miss Ohio.

LIZ

Sweetie –

GEORGE
                    (to everyone:)
So, um, how are the new guests
responding to the place?

CLARK

Well, I got a complaint this morning from
the couple in Number Six. They opened the
Bible in their room to pray, and someone
had underlined all the dirty parts.

JANE

I had to stop a fight in Number Three.
The couple found a magazine someone
had left with some very explicit sex scenes.
The husband was furious, and the wife
wanted a subscription.

GEORGE

What about the two couples with the
cute kids in Numbers Eight and Nine?
They seem happy.

LIZ

Until this morning.

GEORGE

What happened?

LIZ

One couple's son and the other couple's
daughter decided to play doctor.

GEORGE

Were they naked?

LIZ

No. The girl didn't have insurance,
and so the boy refused to examine her.

GEORGE

Any good reports?
>   (after a long beat:)
Anything?

CLARK

Last night I was walking by, and I decided
to see if anything was happening by
the pool, and you know what I saw?

GEORGE

What?

CLARK

Nothing. *Nothing.*

GEORGE

Well that's –

CLARK

At one point, two dragonflies landed on the
pool, shook hands, and flew away. That was it.

GEORGE
>   (to the group:)
Anything else?

JANE

George, is this meeting about over?

GEORGE

Well I –

JANE

'Cause I'm no good at meetings. When you're
in a meeting, you have to sit still and listen

and pretend like you're paying attention,
and that's just not my kind of bondage.

GEORGE

Meeting adjourned.

LIZ

Oh, Jane, George and I want to thank you
again for inviting us to your church. We
thought the service was lovely, didn't we?

GEORGE

Oh, yes. I enjoyed meeting your minister,
and her girl friend, and their kids,
and your minister's sperm donor.

LIZ

And we thought the sermon on tolerance
was very interesting, didn't we?

GEORGE

Oh, yes. I've never heard a sermon before
that quoted both Jesus and Liberace.

JANE

Well, you two are welcome any time.
You'd love our women's group, Liz.

GEORGE

Um –

JANE

And you might want to join our men's group.

GEORGE

Well –

JANE

Don't worry. Two-thirds of the guys are straight.

CLARK

You didn't hear about Marvin?

JANE

Okay, so now it's three-fifths.

Jane exits.

LIZ

This isn't going to work, George.

GEORGE

You're right; I can't go to a church where the minister says, "Blessed are the butch."

LIZ

I mean the Snow White Inn.

GEORGE

But –

LIZ

We should go back to this being the Godiva Inn before it's too late.

GEORGE

It wasn't doing *that* well.

LIZ

I'm sure if we tried, we could –

GEORGE

I'd probably be a failure at that, too.

LIZ

You're not a failure, sweetie.

GEORGE

Liz, get real.

CLARK

Oh, nobody comes to Key West to get real.

GEORGE
(not wanting to hear it)

Clark.

CLARK

I mean, why limit yourself to reality
when life offers so much more?

Clark exits.

LIZ

You're not a failure, George.

GEORGE

Then what am I? I'm not a kid, I'm not special,
and I couldn't find a job in over a year.

LIZ

George, when your company was bought,
they laid off over a thousand people.

GEORGE

Some of them got jobs.

LIZ

Are you still expecting life to be "fair"?
Life has a lot of great qualities, but I don't
think "fair" is something one should expect.

GEORGE

My parents told me life was fair.

LIZ

Your parents also taught you that
good girls don't like sex. It's not true.
Good girls don't like *bad* sex.

GEORGE

Are you saying –

LIZ

I'm just saying, maybe we haven't been
taught everything we need to know.

GEORGE

But I don't know how to run an inn.

LIZ

You can le—

Jane and Clark enter. Clark carries an inflated sex doll.

CLARK

Um, sorry to interrupt, but one of the guests
found this in the garbage and started doing CPR
on it.

Clark tosses it on the couch.

JANE

We also found two girls behind the

storage shed playing Community Clinic.

GEORGE

Communi—

JANE

You don't need insurance.

GEORGE

Good grief.

CLARK

Jane, do you think now'd be a good time
to give George –

JANE

Not yet.

GEORGE

Give me what?

CLARK and JANE

Nothing.

GEORGE

I just – I don't –... I don't know what
to do. Anyone have any suggestions?

CLARK

I know: Let's hold a Mister Nude Key West
contest.

GEORGE

Anybody have any wholesome suggestions?

CLARK

Mister Nude Key West with whipped cream.

JANE

And cherries! If you can find any in Key West.

GEORGE

I, I can't, this whole, I –
      (referring to Clark's eyes:)
I –

      (referring to Liz's outfit,
       with greater emphasis:)
I –

      (referring to the inflated doll,
       with greatest emphasis:)
I –

      (with firm resolve:)
I'm selling this place!

LIZ

George!

GEORGE

And I think I may have already found a buyer.

LIZ

What?

GEORGE

I didn't tell you, but I put out some feelers and –

LIZ

But we agreed it'd be a joint decision.

GEORGE

I know, but –

LIZ

That's not fair.

GEORGE

Well, maybe "fair" isn't something you should
expect!

The lights fade.

SCENE FIVE

A few days later. George is tidying the lobby. As he pats the
back of the couch, something doesn't feel right. He reaches
behind one of the pillows (or cushions) and pulls out a naked
Barbie doll. He pats another pillow, reaches behind it, and
pulls out a Ken doll in a Barbie outfit. He responds like "Will
these annoyances never cease?" He tosses them behind the
desk. The phone rings.

GEORGE
(into the phone:)
Snow White Inn, where the umm –
something something something does
something something something. So,
what can I do for you?...

Another line rings.

GEORGE
Can you hold a second? Thanks.
(switches to the other line, and:)
Snow White Inn, where the – Thank you

for interrupting... Stop yelling!... No, Clark
isn't here... Yes, I'll give him a message...
Can you repeat that without swearing?...
He owes you how much?!... You'll do *what?!*...
Do you mean that literally or figuratively?...
Yes, I'll tell him. 'Bye.
       (switches to the other line, and:)
Thanks for holding... No no no, we *used*
to be the Godiva Inn, but we changed...
No, Roger isn't – I'm, I'm afraid Roger
passed away... So um, did you know him?...
What was he like?... Uh-huh... Uh-huh...
Really?... Well, yes, I knew him – well
actually, we were – we were childhood friends...
Well, you know, you grow up, you go on
different paths... I taught him how to ride
a bike... Uh-huh... Yeah... If, if you,
if you *do* visit Key West again, drop by.
I'd, I'd like to hear more... Thank you. 'Bye.

George hangs up. Liz enters. She's not in a good mood.

Honey, do you know why Jane's car is in the lot?
       (no reply from Liz, then:)
Didn't you say she was going to see a client?
       (no reply from Liz, then:)
That's a really nice dress you're wearing.
       (no reply from Liz, then:)
Nice shoes, too.
       (no reply from Liz, then:)
Excellent accessories.
       (no reply from Liz, then:)
You can at least talk to me.

LIZ
(seething with rage)
Yes, she's seeing a client, and I don't

know why she didn't take her car.

GEORGE
Maybe she has engine problems.

LIZ
(severely)
Not a chance.

GEORGE
And, and, at the risk of being eaten alive,
do you know where Clark put the stapler?

LIZ
Why don't you call him and ask?

GEORGE
I don't want to bother him on his day off.
At least not about a stapler; are you going
to act this way when Starkle shows up?

LIZ
I'll be a pillar of politeness, until he gets
the hell out of here.

GEORGE
Honey, I, I don't blame you for being upset,
but – Do you know how much money
we could make if he wants to buy it?

LIZ
There are more important things
in life than money.

GEORGE
I know, and we can't afford them.

LIZ

Do you want to know what happened to me
the other day, George? Or are you too wrapped
up in your own feelings to give a damn?

GEORGE

I think the correct answer is I want to
know what happened to you the other day.

LIZ

I was walking down the street. And I
felt happy. For no apparent reason.

GEORGE

You know, I, I don't expect you to get
this now, but I'm actually trying to sell
this place for the sake of our marriage.

LIZ

Our marriage? Or *your* idea of
what our marriage should be?

GEORGE

You know, we didn't fight like this in Ohio.

LIZ

That's because the state's motto
is "Don't raise your voice".

GEORGE

Damn it, we don't belong here.

LIZ

Stop saying "we". I love you, George,
but I never gave you my proxy vote.

GEORGE

Okay then, *I* don't belong here. I don't want
to run a hotel that belongs in a brown paper bag!
I don't want to live on an island where Happy
Hour starts at sunrise. I don't want our kids
coming here and seeing –

LIZ

I'm not worried about what they'll see.
I think we raised them with great values.

GEORGE

Those were the only values you could
find in Dayton! I *like* those values and –

LIZ

You don't even know what the values *are* here.

GEORGE

Okay, you like Key West, I like Dayton, we'll
split the difference and move to Atlanta.

LIZ

You know, George, I've met some strange
people at this hotel, some crazy people,
some disgusting people, and a lot of really
nice people. And I don't think the percentages
are that different if you put their clothes on.
I think the only difference between a roomful
of nudists and a roomful of people with clothes
on is that nobody in the roomful of nudists
is fantasizing about wearing clothes.

GEORGE

It's not just the nudity. People come here –

LIZ
To live out their fantasies.

GEORGE
And most of them don't even clean up
afterwards.

LIZ
So what are *your* fantasies, George?
About work, about the future... about sex?
(beat)
If you tell me yours, I'll tell you mine.

GEORGE
I'm not sure I want to hear –

LIZ
C'mon, George, I dare you.
What are your fantasies?... Well?

For a moment, silence. Then:

GEORGE
I... I don't have any.

LIZ
None?

GEORGE
The only fantasies I've ever had were marrying
someone like you, and raising kids like ours.

LIZ
And now?

GEORGE

And now I... I just want my past back.

LIZ

Oh, sweetie. You need some new fantasies.

GEORGE

I know.

LIZ

And here's your chance –

GEORGE

I'm not Roger!

LIZ

I know, but –

GEORGE

I'll never be Roger.

LIZ

Nobody's asking –

GEORGE

I'm not – I'm not – anyone but me...
I'm sorry.

LIZ

I'm not sorry.

GEORGE

Well, you don't spend as much time
with me as I do.

                    LIZ
And I do see how unhappy you are.
But I'm unhappy, too.

                  GEORGE
I know, and, and, and, and... My life would
suck so much more if you weren't in it.

                    LIZ
Oh, Sweetie. You are the number one reason
I'm glad I grew up in Dayton.

They kiss.

               LIZ (cont'd)
Would you like more lobe?

                  GEORGE
Well, it's tempting, but...

               LIZ (cont'd)
You know, that guy from the hotel chain
isn't due here for another half-hour.

                  GEORGE
So?

                    LIZ
Remember before the kids were born,
when we used to have sex without
having to make an appointment?

They kiss again, and they like it. FRED STARKLE, a
businessman, enters. He's good at what he does. He carries a
briefcase and a suitcase.

FRED

So what I've heard about this place is true.

GEORGE

Oh, um, you must be –

FRED

Fred. Fred Starkle.

GEORGE

I'm George Drummond, and this is my wife Liz.

FRED

Fred. Fred Starkle.
      (to George:)
From what I see, you're very lucky
to have her as a wife.

LIZ

Thank you for reminding him.

FRED

So this is what a nudist resort looks like.

GEORGE

Oh, no, it used to be clothing-optional,
but now, just like all the hotels in your chain,
we appeal to a wholesome family crowd.

From off-stage, we hear:

A MALE HOTEL GUEST

(o.s.)

Cuuu-cum-berrrr!

GEORGE

And some fervent vegetarians.

LIZ

So is this your first time in Key West?

FRED

Yes, and I can see how it's gotten its reputation.

What a sexy little island this is.

GEORGE

Oh, no no no. It's really not nearly as sexy
as they say it is. I mean, parts of it are sexy,
but this part isn't sexy at all.

FRED

That's too bad.

GEORGE

I mean, *some* parts of this part are sexy;
just *this* part of this part isn't sexy.

FRED

I see.

LIZ

If you do, you're the only one.

GEORGE

Anyway, let's check you in, and then we'll
show you around the inn, and then we'll
show you around Key West. We'll show you
all the hot spots, although we don't have
to go to the hottest hot spots.

LIZ

Just the tepid hot spots.

GEORGE

Why don't we check you in,
and then we'll show you around.

LIZ

Or would you like to rest a little?

GEORGE

Or maybe you're hungry.

LIZ

What would you like?

GEORGE

Name it. We want your visit here
to be one you'll never forget.

Clark enters. However, one hesitates calling him Clark in his
current look. Dressed in a spectacular gown, heels, a luscious
red wig and sexy make-up, Clark is the essence of
womanhood – and a whole lot more.

CLARK

Hi, hi.

GEORGE

Hi.

LIZ

Hi!

FRED

Hello, there.

CLARK
George, can I see you for a second?

George is still too stunned to move.

LIZ
(to George:)
George.

GEORGE
(startled into movement:)
Um, sure.

CLARK
I really need an advance on my salary.

GEORGE
For how long?

CLARK
Six months to a year.

GEORGE
I really can't discuss it now.

Fred walks over.

FRED
Is there something I can help with?

CLARK
Oh, aren't you the sweetest thing.

FRED
No, but I bet *you* are sweet.

CLARK

Well, I have added to a few men's caloric intake.

FRED

Are you a guest here?

CLARK

No, I work –

GEORGE

Just around the corner.

FRED

What a lucky neighborhood.

GEORGE

Liz, why don't you show Fred to his room?
And give him those papers he wanted.

LIZ

I'll get his key.

FRED

George, you haven't introduced us.

GEORGE

Oh, yes. Fred, this is...

CLARK

Strawberry Fields.

FRED

Fred. Fred Stiffle. Spoojle. *Starkle*.

LIZ
(behind the counter:)
Where *is* that stapler?

CLARK
In the lower left hand drawer, behind
the first aid kit and the duct tape.

GEORGE
Strawberry also helps out here occasionally.

FRED
Really?

CLARK
Whenever my brother Clark, the enormously
useful and underpaid clerk, is sick.

FRED
Well, if you know your way around this place,
perhaps you can give me a tour.

CLARK
Well...

FRED
And then I can show my thanks
by taking you out to dinner.

CLARK
(flattered)
Well.

LIZ
(walking over with the key:)
I don't think that's a –

GEORGE

Oh, good. Here's your room key.
Liz will show you to your room.

LIZ

But –

GEORGE

(to Fred:)
Why don't you just put your stuff
away? Strawberry and I will be here
when you get back, won't she?

CLARK

Anything for my friend George.

LIZ

Fred, I need to talk to Strawberry, too.
Do you mind finding the room by yourself?
It's down the hall, third door on your left.

FRED

No problem. I'm great at finding hotel rooms...
(looking at Clark:)
and sweets.

Fred exits.

GEORGE

Okay, now let's talk advances.

CLARK

He's very good at them.

LIZ

George –

GEORGE

I know what I'm doing. Clark, how
much would you like to be debt-free?

CLARK

I'll do anything, no matter how degrading.

LIZ

For money?!

CLARK

No, just lifestyle.

GEORGE

Clark, if you can get us to close a deal
with Fred, I'll cover your debts.

LIZ

George!

CLARK
(to George:)
You really do hate this place, don't you?

GEORGE

It's just not home. And it'll never be my home.

CLARK

Well –

LIZ

Clark.

CLARK

– what exactly are you asking me to do?

GEORGE
Nothing illegal or immoral.

CLARK
You want me to fluff his pillow?

GEORGE
Just be the way guys like women to be.

CLARK
Act interested when he drones
on and on about himself.

GEORGE
Just show him a nice time.

LIZ
George!

CLARK
How nice?

GEORGE
Nice.

CLARK
A time that's halfway decent.

GEORGE
Exactly.

CLARK
And halfway indecent.

LIZ

Clark –

GEORGE

Don't do anything you wouldn't normally do.

CLARK

That doesn't leave out much.

GEORGE

Don't do anything *I* wouldn't normally do.

CLARK

That doesn't leave in much.

LIZ

George or Clark –

GEORGE

I mean, if I liked men.

CLARK

George, the day you like men they'll make
West Hollywood the nation's capital.

GEORGE

Just use common sense.

CLARK

Do I look like I have that gene?!

LIZ

Clark or George –

GEORGE

You know what I me —

LIZ

Do either of you remember your names?!!!
You may be straight, and you may be
gay, but you're both so... *men*.

GEORGE

I'm just asking him to entertain a client.
It's... It's a standard business practice.

LIZ

And you consider that a higher
moral code than nudism?!

GEORGE

I'm doing this for us.

LIZ

"Us"? *"Us"?!* I don't think I'm in your "us".

Liz exits, very upset.

GEORGE

Liz!

For a moment, both men are silent. Then:

CLARK

I'll do it.

GEORGE

Are you sure it's –

CLARK

But only so I can continue to pursue my art.

Fred enters.

FRED

That's a very nice room. I think
this place has a lot of charm.

GEORGE

In the hands of the right company,
I think it has great potential.

FRED
(looking at Clark:)
In the right hands, I see a lot of great potential,
too.

CLARK

So, Fred – By the way, do you prefer
being called Fred, or Freddy, or   Sugarplum?

FRED

Whatever you'd like.

CLARK

Well then, *Snookums*, how about if
I show you around the inn, and then
we'll take in the highlights of Key West.

FRED

Sounds great. That's a lovely dress,
by the way.

CLARK

Thank you. You know, I once had an
affair with a well-dressed submissive.

FRED

Really?

CLARK
But it turned out he was just a slave to fashion.

Fred and Clark exit.

The lights fade.

SCENE SIX

That night. The lobby is empty. Fred and Clark (as "Strawberry") enter.

CLARK
– and that's why I really think mangos should become our national fruit.

FRED
You are fascinating.

CLARK
Well, thank you.

FRED
You're like Thanksgiving, Christmas and New Year's all together.

CLARK
That's me. A turkey, a goose, and a hangover.

FRED

How'd you like to come to my room?

CLARK
(as in, "Behave yourself")
Oh, now Snookums.

FRED

Maybe a little dip in the hot tub?

CLARK

I don't want to get soggy.

FRED

C'mon. It'll relax you.

CLARK

I think the four margaritas did that.

FRED

C'mon.

CLARK

I don't have a swimsuit.

FRED

At this hour, who cares.

CLARK

Why, Snookums.

FRED

Are you afraid to embrace the erotic?

CLARK

I'd rather lightly hug the erotic

and slowly build from there.

                    FRED
          Just a few minutes in the tub,
          what do you say?

                    CLARK
          I just can't. Not tonight.

                    FRED
          Ohhh, is it that time of the month?

                    CLARK
          Yes. And when I have my period,
          it's an exclamation point! Why don't
          we just sit here for awhile?

                    FRED
          Well, if that's your best offer.

They sit on the couch.

                    FRED (cont'd)
          You know, you are quite a woman.

                    CLARK
          You watch, you learn. So is there anything
          else you'd like to know about the inn?

                    FRED
          You have a stunning face.

                    CLARK
          And you have – fast hands.
                    (pushes Clark's hands away)
          Sooo.... What's your sign?

FRED

Virgo.

CLARK

And your rising?

FRED

You bet I am.

CLARK

I don't think I'll ask for your moon.

FRED

Come here.

Fred makes a play for Clark, but Clark avoids him.

CLARK

Can we slow down a bit?
I am a respectable gal, you know.

FRED

I know the kind of woman you are.

CLARK

Oh, I don't think so.

FRED

You want to be appreciated
for who you really are.

CLARK

Not even close.

FRED

You want men to treat you with respect.

CLARK

I'm just glad when they treat.

FRED

You like feeling manhood between your legs.

CLARK

Oh, I've never lacked for that.

FRED

You know, I'm very well hung.

CLARK

I'm sure.

FRED

You want a look? Seeing is believing.

CLARK

Not in my business – I mean –

FRED

Your "business"? *Business??*

CLARK

Well –

FRED

Are you a... a *"pro"*?

CLARK

Oh, no. I'd like to turn pro someday,
if I ever get really good at it.

                    FRED

You would?

                    CLARK

That's why I like to do it as often
as I can, just to improve my skills.

                    FRED

Improve your –

                    CLARK

I mean, what could be more satisfying than
a night where I can give pleasure to hundreds?

                    FRED

Hundreds?!

                    CLARK

Like today, before I dropped by the inn,
I provided the entertainment at a
Lion's Club luncheon.

                    FRED

This is some island.

                    CLARK

They gave me a nice honorarium,
although between you and me, I was
glad to do it just for the practice.

                    FRED

Really?

                    CLARK

And by the time I finished, I think I can

say that every man there was pleased
he came. And a few women, too.

                    FRED

Oh God.

                    CLARK

Of course, that's because they let me do
my full act. At bars, I only get about
ten minutes, and I can't reveal all my
talents in ten minutes.

                    FRED

I am so turned on.

                    CLARK

A few months ago, I was asked
to perform for charity –

                    FRED

Really?

                    CLARK

It felt so great doing it for the homeless.

                    FRED

I want you!

Fred lunges towards Clark.

                    CLARK

Slow down.

                    FRED

Now!

CLARK

Stop it!

FRED
(pulling out money:)
I'll give you an honorarium!

CLARK
What – what the – did you think –...
Frederick!... Who do you think I am?

FRED
You're not a –

CLARK
I'm a nightclub performer.

FRED
Oh. Oh, I'm sorry. I owe you an apology.

CLARK
Yes, you do.

FRED
I'm very sorry.

CLARK
Okay, that works.

Fred leans in.

FRED
I'm very, very, very –

Fred cops a feel.

CLARK

Hey!

FRED

Is that –... foam rubber?

CLARK

Yes.

FRED

Well, now I know why you didn't want
to get into the hot tub with me.

CLARK

Well...

FRED

Darling, I've been with flat women before.

CLARK

Well, I've considered implants,
but you know...

FRED

You don't need big boobs to be a woman.

CLARK

I just can't afford them.

FRED

I think a woman is more than
the sum of her parts.

CLARK

That's me.

FRED

Strawberry, please, come to my room.

CLARK

Well...

FRED

Let's live dangerously.

CLARK

That's what I think every time I wear heels.

FRED

I look into your eyes, and
you know what I see?

CLARK

Too much mascara?

FRED

I see the beauty of your soul.

CLARK

Holy shit.

FRED

I mean it.

Fred moves closer a bit. Clark moves closer a bit. Fred moves closer a bit.
Clark moves closer a bit. Fred leans in to kiss Clark, and Clark leans wayyyyyy back to avoid him. Fred looks at Clark.

CLARK

Oh, what the hell.

Clark kisses Fred. The kiss becomes mutually passionate.

> FRED
> Would you please visit my room?

> CLARK
> (Clark voice:)
> Why, is there something wrong with it, I mean –
> (as Strawberry:)
> Yes, I'd like that.

They start to leave.

> FRED
> You know, you have a great ass.

Fred grabs Clark's ass.

> CLARK
> And you have a fine grasp of the obvious.

They exit.

The lights fade.

SCENE SEVEN

The next morning. Liz is at the front desk. She's dressed casually but nicely, like she'd fit in perfectly in Key West. She rummages for something behind the desk... and discovers naked Barbie and transvestite Ken. She looks at them a moment, and then, as if they've triggered something, she imagines a conversation between them:

LIZ

(as herself, to Ken:)
Gee, Ken, I like the way you look.
(as Ken, to Barbie:)
I like the way you look too, Barbie.
I've known you fifty years, and
you haven't sagged a bit.
(as Barbie:)
Ken, why are people so hung up
about naked bodies?
(as Ken:)
I don't know, Barbie. Of course, I don't
have genitals. To be honest, I've never
understood what you see in me.
(as Barbie:)
You have lots of fine qualities, Ken.
You never lose your smile.
(as Ken:)
Yeah. I think my face was the inspiration for
Botox.
(as Barbie:)
Oh, Ken.
(as Ken:)
I do love you, Barbie. I'm sorry if I can't
be as much of a man as you deserve.
(as Barbie, but with
a little Liz mixed in:)
I love you too, Ken. I just wish there was
more of a correlation between love and… and…
(Liz's voice:)
happiness.

The phone rings. Liz puts away the Ken and Barbie dolls and
answers it.

LIZ
(without enthusiasm)
Snow White Inn, where –... Oh, who cares.

Liz hangs up. Jane enters, in her handyman outfit.

JANE
So how's it going?

LIZ
I'd feel better if I had heard from Clark.

JANE
I saw him.

LIZ
Where?

JANE
He's using an empty room to change.

LIZ
You mean he was here all night?

JANE
Judging from the pound of makeup
still on his face, that's my guess.
(then:)
Of course, some of it *was* smeared.

LIZ
Oh, God. Jane, what – what am I supposed
to do? I don't want to leave. I can't make
George stay. I don't know what to do.
In Dayton I *always* knew what to do...
I think some couples have dull marriages

just so they know what to do.

JANE

My marriage wasn't dull. I would've killed for
dull.

LIZ

Your ex sounds like such a creep.
Why did you ever fall for him?

JANE

Well, he took an interest in me, which put him
apart from most men. And after awhile, he took
me for granted, dismissed everything I had to
say, used me for sex, and I thought, I've finally
met a guy who treats me like a woman.

LIZ

But –

JANE

And when you don't feel like one, you
settle for any reassurance you can get.

LIZ

Well, I think you're one hell of a woman.

JANE

Ditto.

LIZ

You know, yesterday I was showing Margaret
the welder how to do an oil change.

JANE

No kidding. That's wonderful.

George enters, unseen by the women.

>   LIZ
> I've grown so much in the short time I've
> been here, in ways I never could've imagined.

>   JANE
> Well, my friends think you're top notch,
> and most of them have many notches.

>   LIZ
> Margaret was *so* into it. She lubed her
> chassis in no time.

>   JANE
> I knew once you learned the technique,
> you'd be a great teacher.

>   LIZ
> She was so pleased, she showed me
> how to use her torch.

>   GEORGE
> Oh my god!

>   LIZ
> George!

George rushes up to Liz, gets on his knees, and grabs her legs.

>   GEORGE
> Please don't become a lesbian! I love you.
> I love making love to you. I want to keep
> making love to you the rest of my life.
> Don't become a lesbian!!!

LIZ

George?

GEORGE

I'll buy you a torch!!!

LIZ

What makes you think I've become a lesbian?

GEORGE

It's, it's, it's tool belts, and and lubrication,
and "ways I never could've imagined" and and

–

JANE

George, I taught your wife how
to maintain your Buick.

GEORGE

And what is *that* a euphemism for?

LIZ

Maintaining our Buick.

GEORGE

The, the Buick we drove here?

LIZ

That's right.

GEORGE

The one that's been driving really smoothly

lately?

LIZ

Uh-huh.

GEORGE

Oh... I thought –... I heard –...
(to Jane:)
I must be the biggest jerk you ever met.

JANE

If it makes you feel better,
you didn't even make the Top Ten.

Clark enters, dressed as Clark.

JANE (cont'd)

Good morning, lover boy.

CLARK

Please, not so loud. Does anyone
have either an aspirin or tequila?

LIZ

I'll get you an aspirin.

GEORGE

Are you okay?

CLARK

Well, you know how it is. You go out
and live it up and have fun, fun, fun,
and then you wake up – *and you're in
a man's body!*... I never get used to it.

GEORGE

So how'd it go?

CLARK

It went fine until he started snoring.

GEORGE

Did you and he –

CLARK

Welllll...

GEORGE

I didn't ask you to –

CLARK

I know.

GEORGE

You didn't have to –

CLARK

I know.

GEORGE

So did he and you, did he, did you –

CLARK

You want me to draw you a picture?

GEORGE

That's okay.

Liz hands Clark an aspirin and a cup of water.

LIZ

Go ahead. Draw me one.

GEORGE

Liz!

LIZ

I like the visual arts.

CLARK

Well let's see, he took me to dinner, and he
filled me with compliments and champagne,
both of which went to my head. So I drank
a lot of water to balance the alcohol. But
then I needed salt to balance the water.
So we had some margaritas. And then
we went for a moonlit walk.

GEORGE

There was no moon out last night.

CLARK

I believe *I* have the paint brush! And we
came back here, and ended up in his room,
and he told me he liked a woman with big
feet, and that just turned me to mush.

GEORGE

Oh god.

CLARK

A mashed mushy mosh pit of mush.
So we turned the lights down low, very low,
and I gave him the kind of night he's always
wanted a woman to give him.

GEORGE

But did he – did you –

CLARK

He fell asleep, and, like so many divas,
I gave more pleasure than I received.

GEORGE

Did you talk about the deal?

LIZ

No. I don't want to hear this part.

GEORGE

Liz!

LIZ

We could make this place work!

GEORGE

I can't.

LIZ

But *we* could!

GEORGE

I don't think I'm in your "we"!

LIZ

Damn it, George... the hardest part of
being married to you... is that I'm the
only one of us who believes in you.

GEORGE

Liz.

LIZ

Keep away from me.

Liz exits.

                    GEORGE
                (following her:)
Liz!

                    JANE
                (stopping him:)
Give her some time, George.

                    GEORGE
But –

                    JANE
I'll talk to her.

                    GEORGE
But –

                    JANE
Trust me. I understand women.
I am one, *and* I date them.

Jane exits.

                    GEORGE
                (to Clark:)
So... so did he say anyth —

                    CLARK
Well, he was evasive mostly, but since we
did end the evening with him being putty in
my hands, and then kind of not like putty –

GEORGE

Okay! Thank you for your delicacy in
answering.

CLARK

Funny. Last night I... I...
(surprisingly vulnerable)
I kinda felt like a delicacy.

Fred enters, with his suitcase and briefcase.

FRED

Good morning, everyone.

GEORGE

Good morning, Fred.

Fred stares at Clark.

CLARK

Hi, I'm Clark the clerk. Strawberry's brother.

FRED

There's, there's quite a resemblance.

CLARK

Well, our parents were also brother and
sister, so there was a very limited gene pool.

GEORGE

So, Fred, did you have a nice time last night?

CLARK

Yeah, did you?

FRED
Between us guys, I had *fun*.

CLARK
Between us guys, I knew you would.

FRED
Well, George, I had a great visit.

GEORGE
Can I take you to breakfast?

FRED
Nah, I moved my flight up and –

GEORGE
Can I drive you to th—

FRED
That's okay. I called a cab.

GEORGE
I was hoping we could –

FRED
George, I did the math.

GEORGE
We can negotiate.

FRED
George, there are already big hotel chains and lots of little B & B's on this island. If a family wants to come here, they have enough choices.

GEORGE

But –

FRED

And this place is cute, but it doesn't have
many rooms. It's too expensive to run for
the economy customer, and it certainly will
never be chic enough for the luxury class.

GEORGE
(putting it together:)
But... but didn't you know all this
before you got here?

FRED

Well, I didn't say this island lacked attractions.

GEORGE

Ohh... I see.

FRED

It's business, George.

GEORGE

Yeah. Business. Is, is there anything
you'd like me to tell Strawberry?

FRED

Oh, you know, the usual crap.

CLARK

What?!

FRED

Sorry. I – I mean, your sister's nice.

CLARK

"Nice"?! Last night you said she was *special*.

FRED

How would you know?

CLARK

It's a small island.

FRED

Well, I was pretty drunk –

CLARK

You weren't that drunk.

FRED

How would you know?

CLARK

It's a small island.

FRED

Apparently.

CLARK

And on a small island, sometimes when
a girl has a date, she tells one friend
about it, who tells one friend, who tells
another friend, who tells me *everything*.

Liz and Jane enter.

LIZ

Oh, Mr. Starkle. I'm glad you're still here.
The cleaning woman found this in your room.

Liz hands Fred a wedding ring.

> FRED
>
> Oh, um, thanks.

> JANE
>
> In case you've forgotten which finger
> it goes on, it's this one.
> > (Jane gives Fred the finger.)
> Oops, off by one.

> CLARK
>
> You're married?!

> FRED
>
> What do you care?

> CLARK
>
> You never told her you were married.

> FRED
>
> I paid for dinner!

> CLARK
>
> *Mister Starkle, there are some things*
> *my sister doesn't do!*

> FRED
>
> Wanna bet?

Clark takes his cup of water and tosses the water in Fred's face.

> FRED (cont'd)
>
> What's the matter with you?!

CLARK
No, what's the matter with *you*?!

GEORGE
Um –

FRED
(to Clark:)
Look, I'm sorry but, but you know
how guys are.

JANE
What the hell kind of excuse is that?!

FRED
I –

JANE
It's people like you who give
heterosexual men a bad name!

FRED
What?

JANE
Did you ever stop to think for one second
about how your actions reflect upon
the heterosexual community?!

FRED
I have no idea what you're –

JANE
With examples like you, I'm surprised
they let heterosexual men marry! Or serve

in the armed forces! Or teach our kids!

                    GEORGE
Jane.

                    JANE
Don't stop me; I'm just revving up.
          (to Fred:)
We're no angels down here. We screw
up as much as anybody. But at least
we know that, that, that...
          (shifting from anger to the
          tender pain underneath)
that heartache is a sexually transmitted disease.

A beat. George checks his watch.

                    GEORGE
And once again, it's just 9:30.

Off-stage, we hear a car horn honk.

                    FRED
There's my cab. George, I'm sorry it
didn't work out, but, well, best of luck.

Fred extends his hand. George doesn't take it.

                    GEORGE
Fred, there's – there's something
you should know about Strawberry.

                    FRED
What?

                         CLARK
          If you got her pregnant, we'll track you down!

Another car honk.

                          FRED
             Well, it's been fun. 'Bye.

Fred exits.

                        GEORGE
                  (calling after him:)
             Nice meeting you... shithead!

                         CLARK
                 (to the rest of the room:)
             Did George just utter a profanity?

                          JANE
             Yep.

Clark gives Jane five dollars.

                           LIZ
             Can, can you imagine how he'd feel if
             he found out the truth about Strawberry?

                         CLARK
             Oh, he knew.

                        GEORGE
             What do you mean?

                         CLARK
             They always know.

_____

GEORGE

But then –

CLARK

They just don't let themselves know they know.

GEORGE

I feel like I have a compass which says
North, South, East and West, and I've
entered a universe with completely
different directions.

JANE

I'm sorry it didn't work out, George.

GEORGE

Well, to be honest, I'm, I'm, I'm not sorry.

LIZ

You're not?

GEORGE

(mostly to Clark:)
All night I couldn't sleep; I, I kept thinking
about what I asked you do – and why.
It just seemed so... I would never ask
me to do what I asked you to do.

CLARK

It was an adventure.

GEORGE

Clark, maybe you didn't go against
your morals. But I went against mine.

CLARK

It's really o—

GEORGE

No, it's not. Since the moment I've arrived, you've been friendly and helpful and considerate, and I've been judgmental and selfish and... and unchristian. I'm sorry.

CLARK

What I don't get is, you seem like basically a decent guy. Why didn't you talk to your brother for all those years?

JANE

You don't talk to your brother.

CLARK

My brother's an asshole.

JANE

But –

CLARK
(to George and Liz:)
My brother stole my college boy friend and they eloped to Massachusetts.

LIZ

Well, that stinks.

CLARK

I don't know if being gay is genetic or environmental or what, but I do know this: Being an asshole is a lifestyle choice.

I don't see George being an asshole.
Were you, George?

GEORGE

I, I don't think so.

CLARK

You're just homophobic.

GEORGE

I'm not hom– well, I probably am, but –
but, you see, I, I always obeyed the rules.
I always did what I was told. I always *thought*
what I was told. Roger broke every rule,
and did what he wanted, and thought what
he wanted, and said what he wanted, and,
and he was always so popular. And daring.
And successful. And I, I didn't compare.
It's not so much that I disapproved of him.
          (embarrassed and open)
I just hated him.

CLARK
          (to Jane:)
Should I?

JANE

Definitely

LIZ

Should you what?

Clark goes to the front desk and retrieves a manila envelope.

CLARK
                (first to Liz, but ending on George:)
        Before he died, Roger wrote you
        a letter, and he left it to us to decide
        whether or not to give it to you.

Clark takes a letter-sized envelope out of the manila envelope
and gives it to George.

CLARK
        Here. Read it in good health.

George opens the envelope and begins to read the letter. He's
moved.

LIZ
        Preferably aloud.

GEORGE
        Well...

JANE
        Enunciate.

CLARK
        We're all ears, among other delightful body
        parts.

GEORGE
        "Dear George, I hope you and Liz are enjoying
        Key West. If not, it might help to know that
        when I came here, my first impulse was to
        run. Fortunately, my second impulse was
        to ignore my first impulse.
                "I'm sorry you were so uncomfortable
        with my life. Despite appearances, it took

me years to find a life I was comfortable with, and I wish the same to you and to everyone on this planet. I know I wasn't always the best brother; I didn't have the patience to watch you work through your prejudices, and I lacked the confidence that you could. That was *my* prejudice. If it makes you feel better, there were a lot of times I wasn't there for me, either. The greatest joy of having friends is knowing people who love you even when you don't love yourself.

"I'm very proud of the life I built here. If you still want to get to know me, get to know my world, especially the people in my world. Despite my death, I like to think I live through them.

"I'm sorry we never got to know each other better. Mostly, I regret all those years I didn't feel safe loving you. The best part of dying is that it makes fear seem so insignificant.

"Love, Roger.

"P.S. Thanks for teaching me how to ride a bike."

LIZ

That's quite a letter.

GEORGE

Yeah.

JANE

Actually, it's one of four.

LIZ

What?

Clark takes three other letter envelopes out of the manila envelope.

CLARK
Roger wrote four letters. One was to be given to George if he was so hostile and obnoxious that we wanted to get rid of him.

GEORGE
Well, I'm honored you didn't give me that one.

CLARK
One was if I found George sexually attractive – sorry, George.

GEORGE
I can handle it.

CLARK
And one was if we found George basically decent but hopelessly confused.
That's the one I gave you.

LIZ
What about letter number four?

CLARK
Oh, this was for if you turned out to be surprisingly kinky and wanted a list of all the decadent places on the island.

Liz takes that envelope.

GEORGE
Um –

                    LIZ
I just want to be prepared in case
anyone wants recommendations, okay?

                  GEORGE
I haven't known what to think since 9:30.

                    LIZ
Sweetie, I was really touched by what you
said before when you were on your knees.

                  CLARK
Oh, I missed something good, didn't I?

                  JANE
Yep.

                  GEORGE
          (to Liz:)
I just want –... I just...

                    LIZ
What do you want, George? Down deep,
more than anything, what do you want?

George looks at Liz and kisses her passionately.

                  CLARK
Boy, they're not just heterosexuals,
they're fanatics.

                  JANE
Maybe there *are* fun people in Ohio.

The phone rings.

GEORGE
Clark, will you get that?

CLARK
How shall I answer it?

George walks to the phone, thinks a second, and picks it up.

GEORGE
(into the phone:)
Godiva Inn. Where love in all forms
is fully caressed; and the owner is
humbled, even when dressed.

George begins to listen to the caller, as...

The lights fade.

THE END

Made in the USA
Middletown, DE
22 September 2021

48905804R00076